MW01591475

Faith of Our Fathers

Celebrating Our American Heritage

Written and Arranged for Senior Adult Choirs

by *Marty Parks*

LILLENAS
PUBLISHING COMPANY

Copyright © 2003 by PsalmSinger Music, Box 419527, Kansas City, MO 64141.
All rights reserved. Litho in U.S.A.

lillenas.com

Contents

My Country, 'Tis of Thee

with

This Is My Country, America

SAMUEL F. SMITH

Thesaurus Musicus
Arranged by Marty Parks

Arr. © 2003 by PsalmSinger Music (BMI). All rights reserved.
Administered by The Copyright Company, 1025 16th Avenue South, Nashville, TN 37212.

PLEASE NOTE: Copying of this product is NOT covered by CCLI licenses. For CCLI information call 1-800-234-2446.

15 *Divisi*

Of thee I sing: Land where my fa - thers died,

Divisi

Fm | Eb/Bb | Bb7 | Eb | **15** Gm | Cm

Land of the Pil - grims' pride, From ev - 'ry____

Fm | Bb7 | **19** Eb

rit.

22 Faster, bright and energetic ♩ = ca. 120

moun - tain-side Let____ free - dom ring!

Eb | Bb7/F Eb/G | Ab | Eb/Bb Bb7 | **22** Eb

rit.

Faster

CD: 2

"This Is My Country, America"
Unison

This is my coun - try, A - mer - i - ca!

This is the land of the

*Words and Music by MARTY PARKS. Copyright © 2003 by PsalmSinger Music (BMI). All rights reserved. Administered by The Copyright Company, 1025 16th Avenue South, Nashville, TN 37212.

50

Divisi

This is_____ the land, rich-ly blest by_____ God's

Divisi

50 B♭   D m/B   C   B♭2 C/B♭   A   A7/C#

54

hand, Where the stars and the stripes still

D m   D m/C   **54** B♭   A m   D m/A   G m   B♭/C

CD: 3

58 *Unison* *mf*

wave.   We've learned from

F2   F   F/E♭   **58** D♭

mf

10

mor - row   Is   in   the   One   who

led   us   in   the   past._____

CD: 4

A/E   F°7   F♯m   Bm/D

Bm   A/C♯   Bm/D   B7/D♯   Esus   E   E/D   Csus   C

8vb - - - - -

This   is   my   coun - try,   A - mer - i - ca!

Unison

Unison

F   FM7   B♭/C   Dm/C   B♭/C   C/F   F

NARRATOR *(without music)*: Welcome, everybody! Welcome to a celebration of America! We're here to pay tribute to the greatest nation this world has ever known. And we're here to honor God, the Author of liberty, the One who makes it all possible.

You know, music has always played a vital part in our nation's history– in wartime or in peace; in seasons of poverty or prosperity; in tragedy and in triumph. And so, today (tonight) we continue that legacy with music: songs of our great country, songs of our mighty God. Some old, some new…all of them just right for our celebration. *(Music begins)*

But watch out– you just might find yourself singing along!

This Land Is Your Land

with

I'm a Yankee Doodle Dandy

Words and Music by
WOODIE GUTHRIE
Arranged by Marty Parks

Copyright 1956 (Renewed) 1958 (Renewed) 1970 (Renewed) Ludlow Music, Inc.,
New York, NY (BMI). All rights reserved. Used by permission.

PLEASE NOTE: Copying of this product is NOT covered by CCLI licenses. For CCLI information call 1-800-234-2446.

19

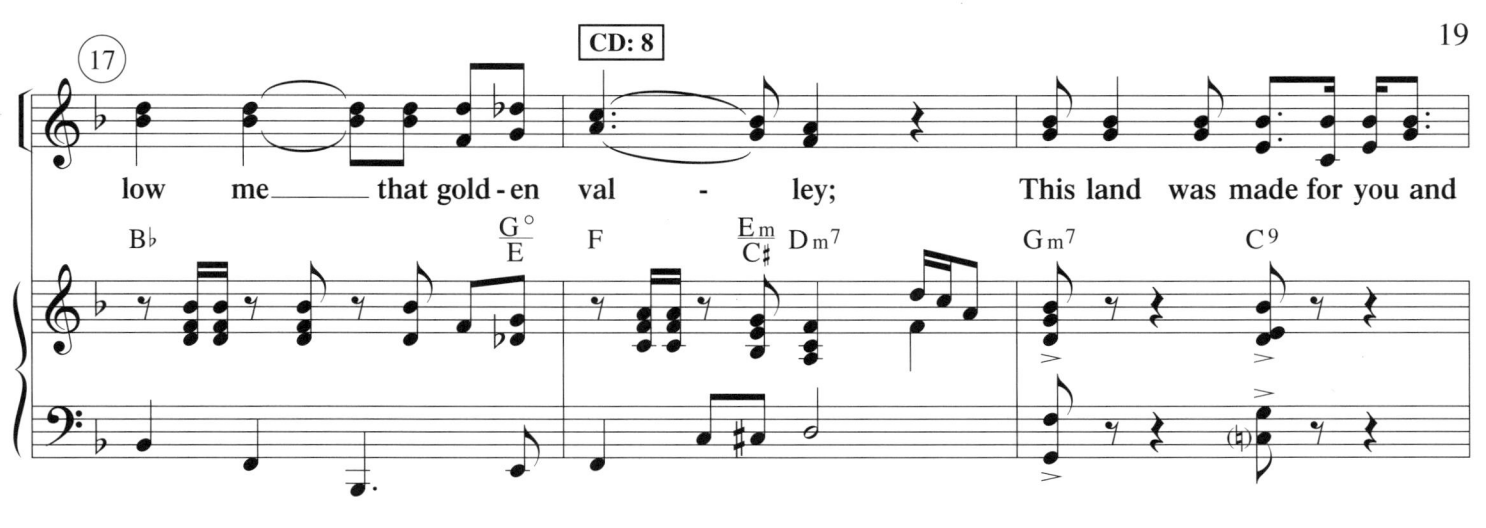

low me_____ that gold-en val - ley; This land was made for you and

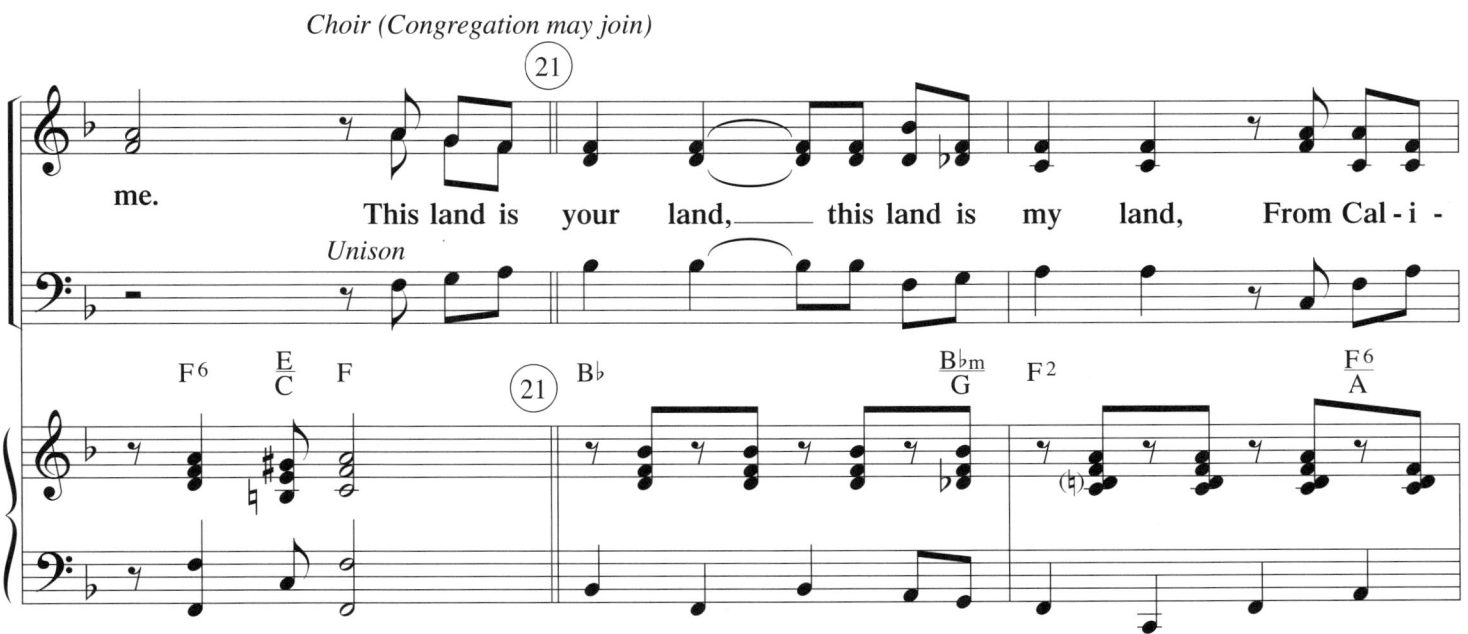

Choir (Congregation may join)

me. This land is your land,_____ this land is my land, From Cal-i-

for - nia_____ to the New York is - land; From the red-wood

22

*"I'm a Yankee Doodle Dandy"

I'm a Yan-kee Doo-dle Dan - dy, A
Yan - kee Doo-dle, do or die; A real live neph-ew of my
Un - cle Sam, Born on the Fourth of Ju - ly. I've

*Words and Music by GEORGE M. COHAN. Arr. © 2003 by PsalmSinger Music (BMI). All rights reserved. Administered by The Copyright Company, 1025 16th Avenue South, Nashville, TN 37212.

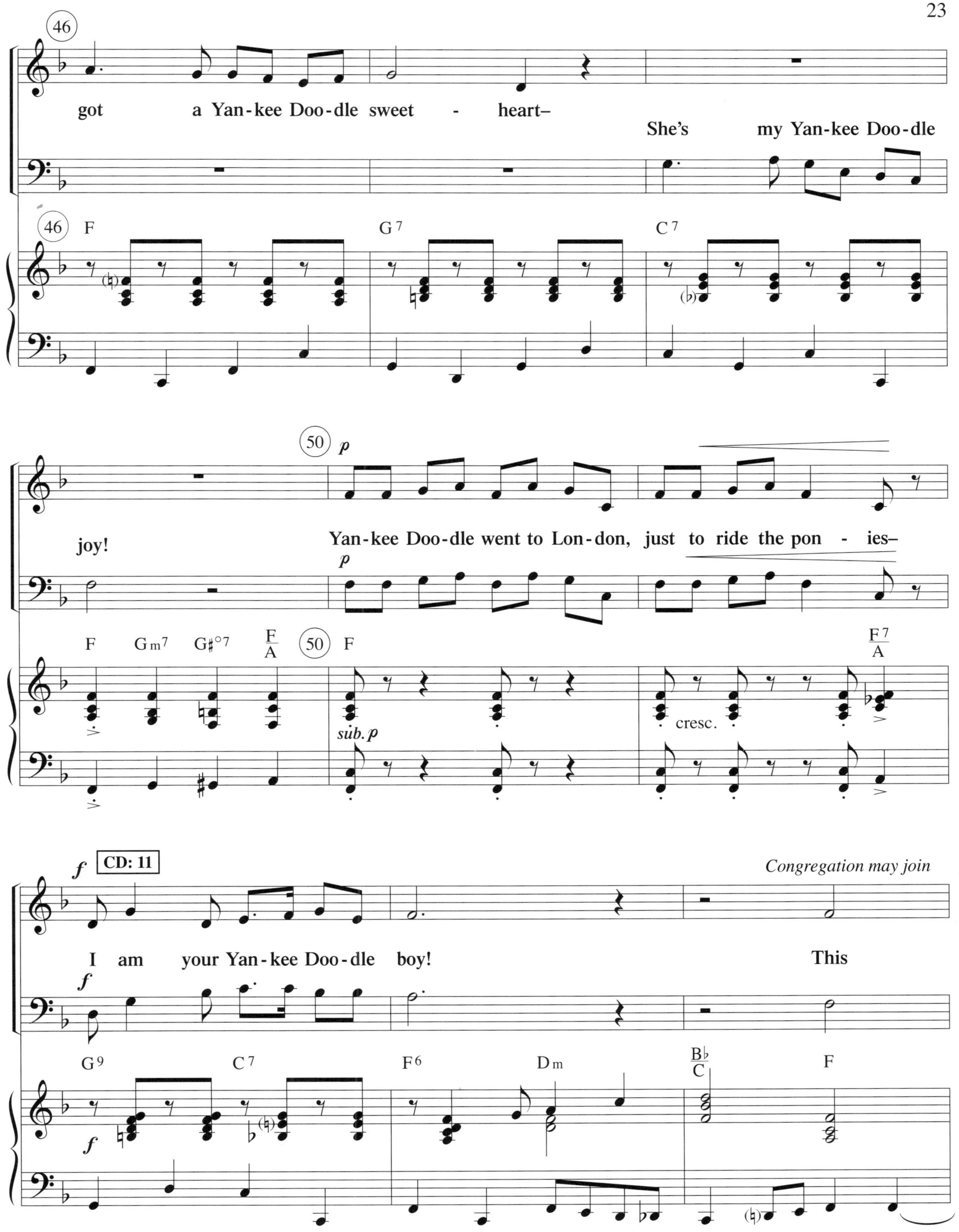
46
got a Yan-kee Doo-dle sweet - heart–
She's my Yan-kee Doo-dle
46
F
G 7
C 7
50
p
joy!
Yan-kee Doo-dle went to Lon-don, just to ride the pon - ies–
p
F
Gm7
G♯°7
F/A
50
F
F7/A
sub. p
cresc.
f
CD: 11
Congregation may join
I am your Yan-kee Doo-dle boy!
This
f
G9
C7
F6
Dm
B♭/C
F
f

NARRATOR *(without music)*: Well, I don't know about you, but that sure makes me proud; proud of my country, proud of its spirit, proud of its flag and all it stands for. Won't you join me by standing and pledging our allegiance to this great flag of the United States?

EVERYONE: I pledge allegiance to the flag of the United States of America; and to the Republic for which it stands, one nation under God, indivisible with liberty and justice for all.

NARRATOR: *(after seating congregation, music begins)*: "One nation under God"; I love that phrase. It reminds me of the words of Psalm 90: "Lord, you have been our dwelling place throughout all generations. Before the mountains were born or you brought forth the earth and the world, from everlasting to everlasting you are God. *(Psalm 90:1-2 NIV)*

God of Strength and God of Power

with
O God, Our Help in Ages Past

DEBRA GRUBBS

MARTY PARKS
Arranged by Marty Parks

Copyright © 2003 by PsalmSinger Music (BMI). All rights reserved.
Administered by The Copyright Company, 1025 16th Avenue South, Nashville, TN 37212.

PLEASE NOTE: Copying of this product is NOT covered by CCLI licenses. For CCLI information call 1-800-234-2446.

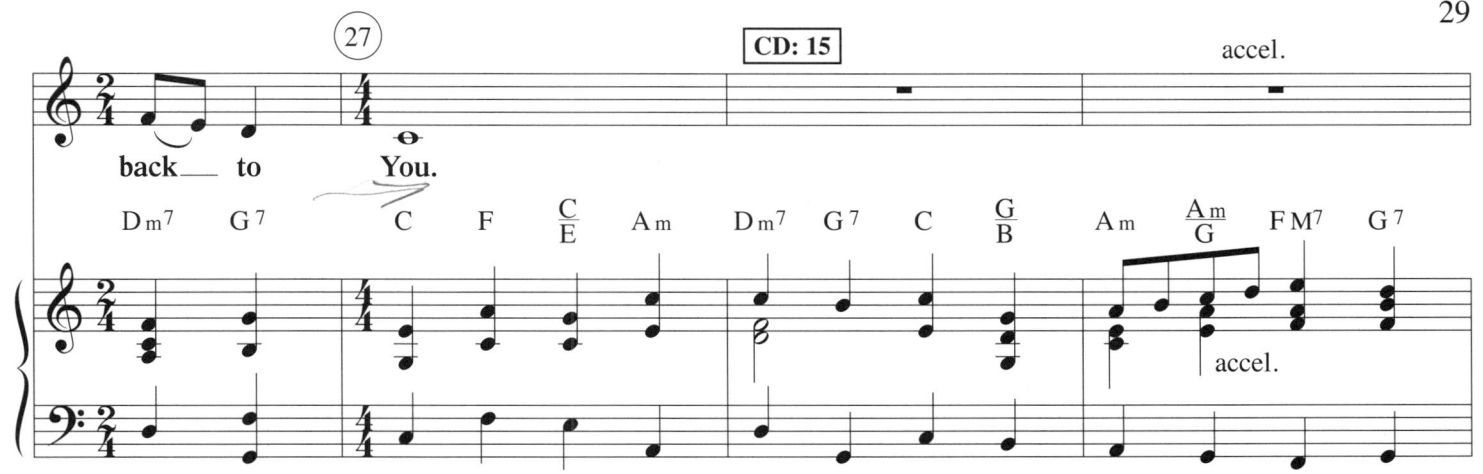

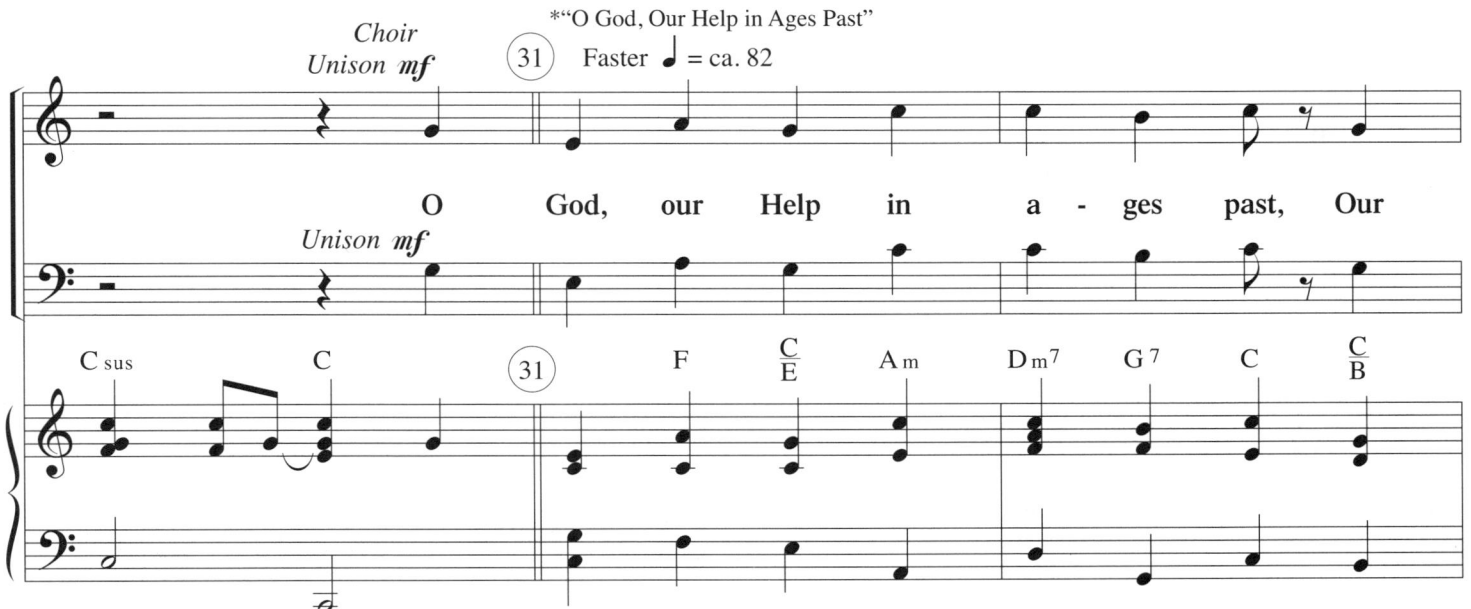

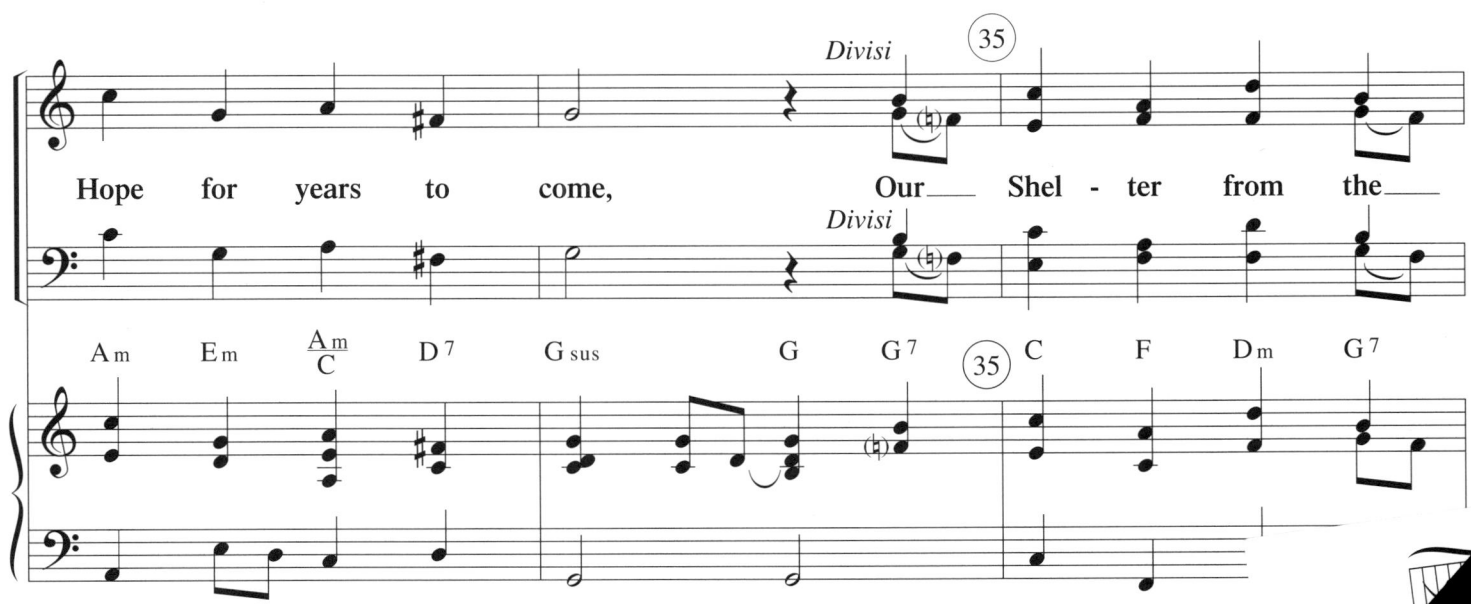

*Words by ISAAC WATTS; Music by WILLIAM CROFT. Arr. © 2003 by PsalmSinger Music (BMI). All rights reserved. Administered by The Copyright Company South, Nashville, TN 37212.

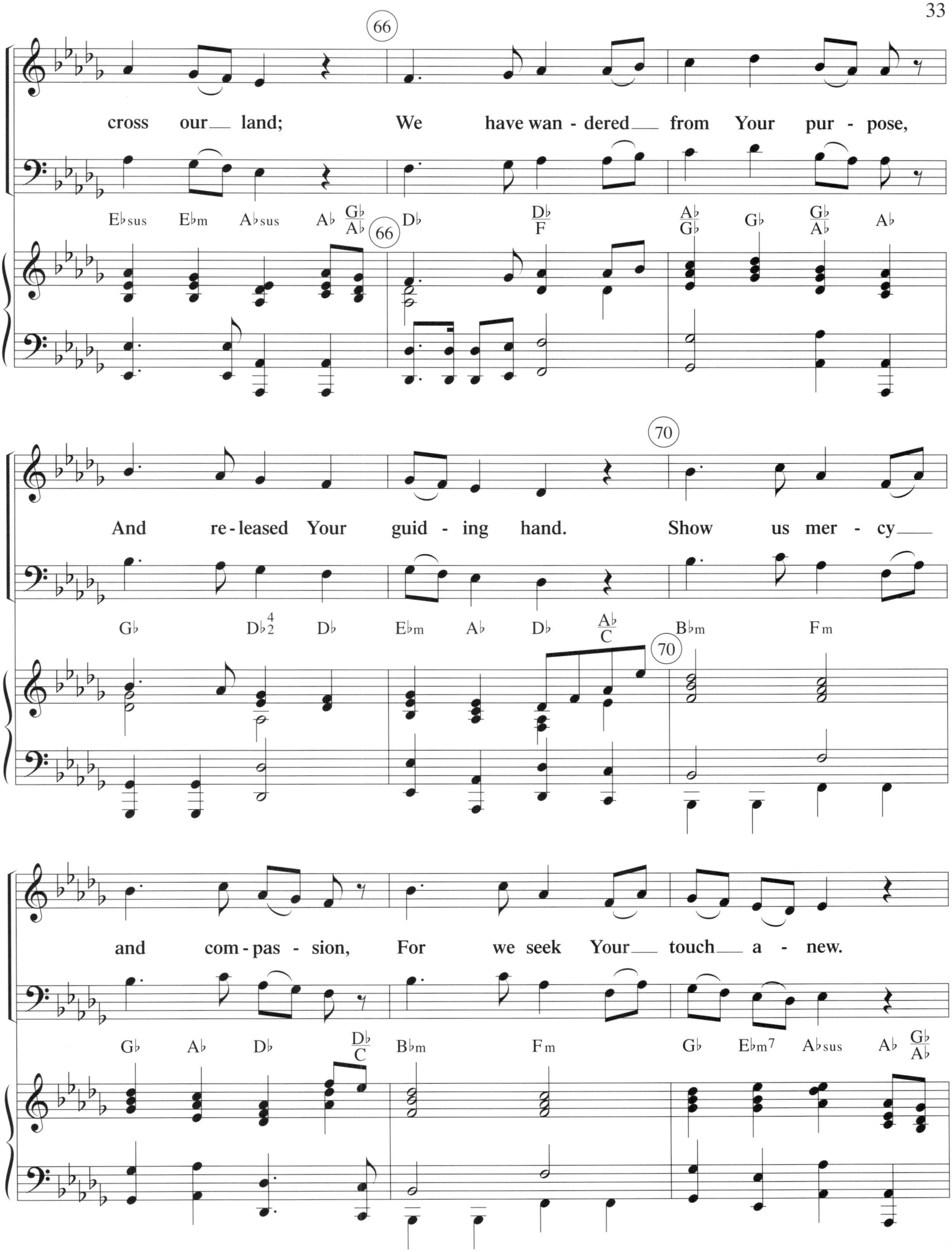
66
cross our land; We have wan - dered from Your pur - pose,
E♭sus E♭m A♭sus A♭ G♭/A♭ D♭ D♭/F A♭/G♭ G♭ G♭/A♭ A♭
70
And re-leased Your guid - ing hand. Show us mer - cy
G♭ D♭4/2 D♭ E♭m A♭ D♭ A♭/C B♭m Fm
and com-pas - sion, For we seek Your touch a - new.
G♭ A♭ D♭ D♭/C B♭m Fm G♭ E♭m7 A♭sus A♭ G♭/A♭

Breathe on us Your___ heal - ing Spir - it, Bring our na - tion

back___ to You. O God, our Help,

Bring us back to You!___

Hear Our Prayer

Words and Music by
MARTY PARKS
Arranged by Marty Parks

NARRATOR: "If my people, who are called by my name, will humble themselves and pray and seek my face and turn from their wicked ways, then will I hear from heaven and will forgive their sin and will heal their land." (2 Chronicles 7:14 NIV)

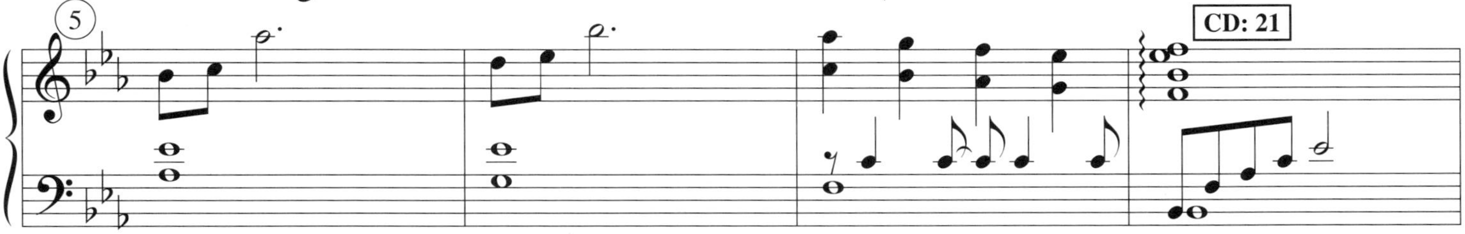

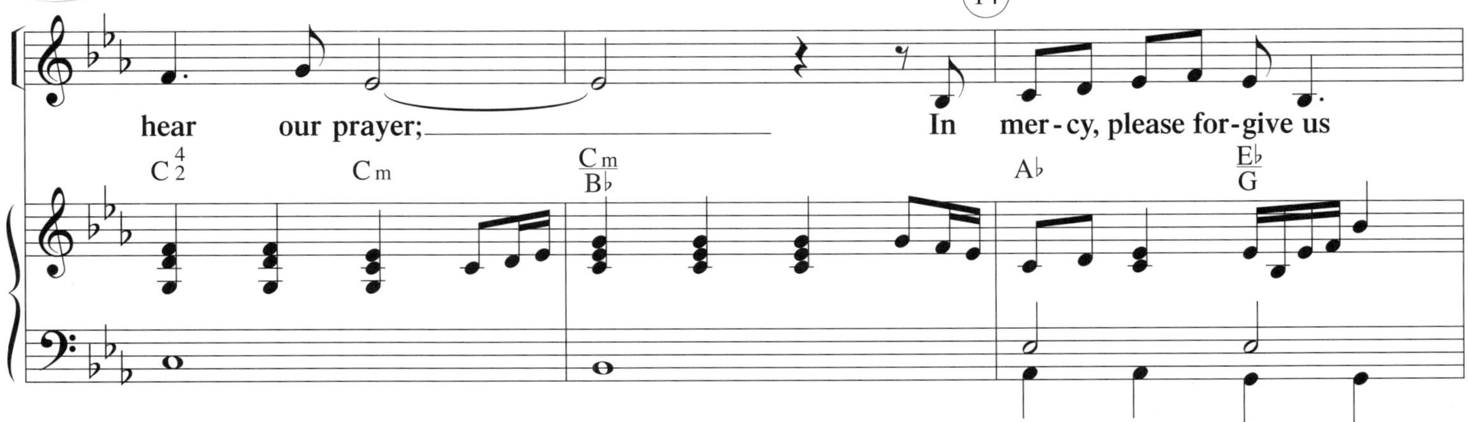

Hear our prayer, O Fa-ther, hear our prayer;_____ In mer-cy, please for-give us

Copyright © 2003 by PsalmSinger Music (BMI). All rights reserved.
Administered by The Copyright Company, 1025 16th Avenue South, Nashville, TN 37212.

PLEASE NOTE: Copying of this product is NOT covered by CCLI licenses. For CCLI information call 1-800-234-2446.

CD: 22
mf
as Your bless - ing we share.
And
Unison mf
Fm9
B♭sus
B♭
A♭/B♭
B♭
18
heal our land,
O Fa - ther,
Divisi
heal our land;
E♭2
E♭
B♭/D
B♭6/D
C 4 2
Cm
mf
22
And grant to us Your vis - ion,
And the cour - age to
Cm/B♭
A♭
E♭/G
Fm9

stand.

26

Cour - age to stand.

Divisi

Your pre-cepts are ho - ly and

Unison

G sus   G $\frac{F^2}{G}$ G   26   A♭   A♭M7 $\frac{B♭}{A♭}$

3   3

Unison

right,

And Your Word gives ra - di - ant light!

So

$\frac{E♭}{G}$ $\frac{E♭sus}{F}$ E♭   A♭   A♭M7 $\frac{B♭}{A♭}$ Gm   C sus   C7

3

30

Divisi

hear   our prayer,   Lord, hear our prayer.

Divisi

30   Fm $\frac{E♭}{G}$ $\frac{Fm}{A♭}$ N.C. $\frac{Fm^7}{B♭}$ B♭7   E♭

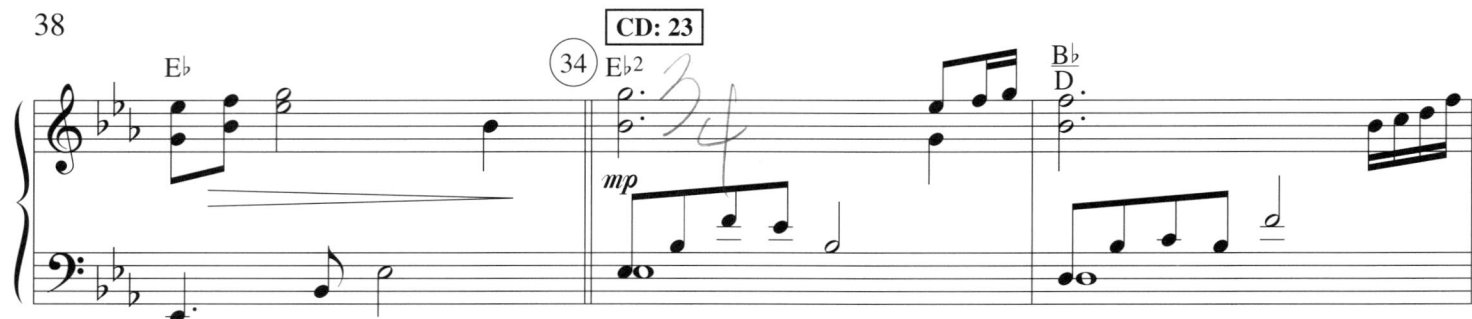

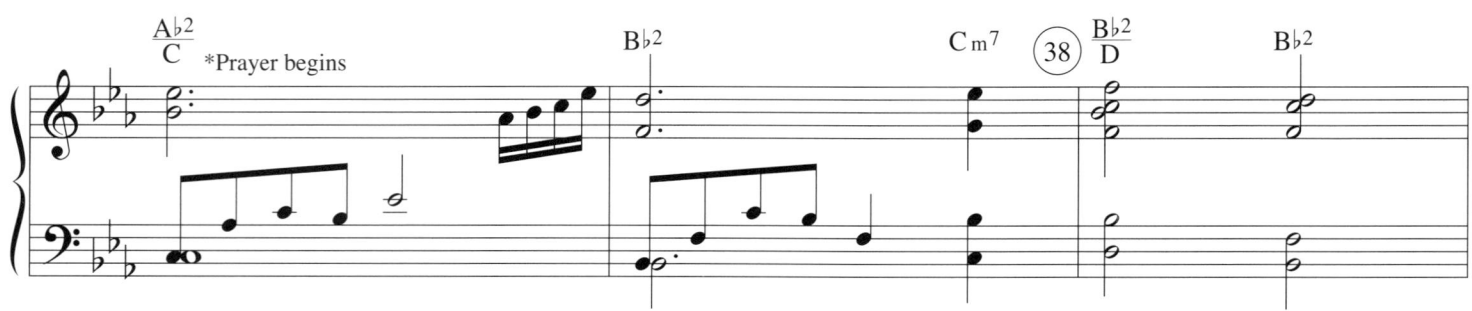

*CHOIR AND CONGREGATION: Our Father, who art in Heaven, hallowed be Thy name. Thy kingdom come, Thy will be done on earth as it is in Heaven. Give us this day our daily bread; and forgive us our debts as we forgive our debtors. And lead us not into temptation, but deliver us from evil. For Thine is the Kingdom and the Power and the Glory forever. Amen.

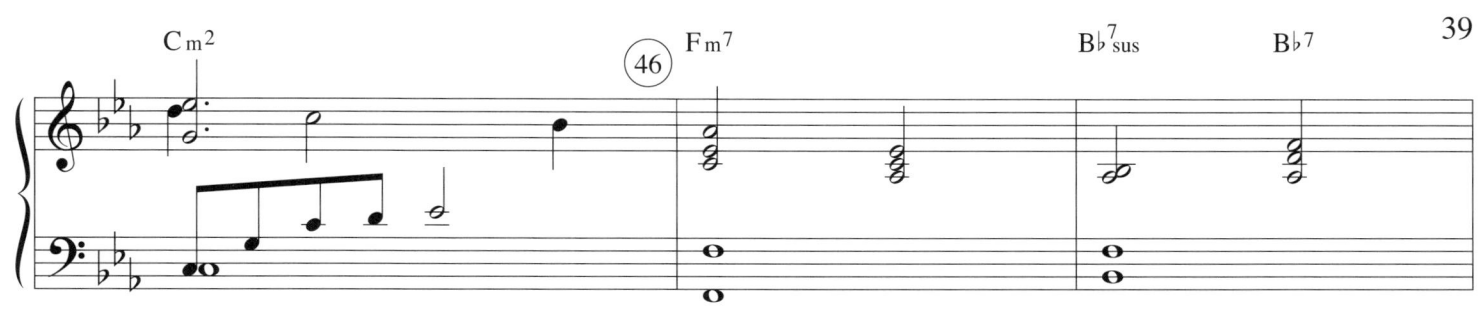

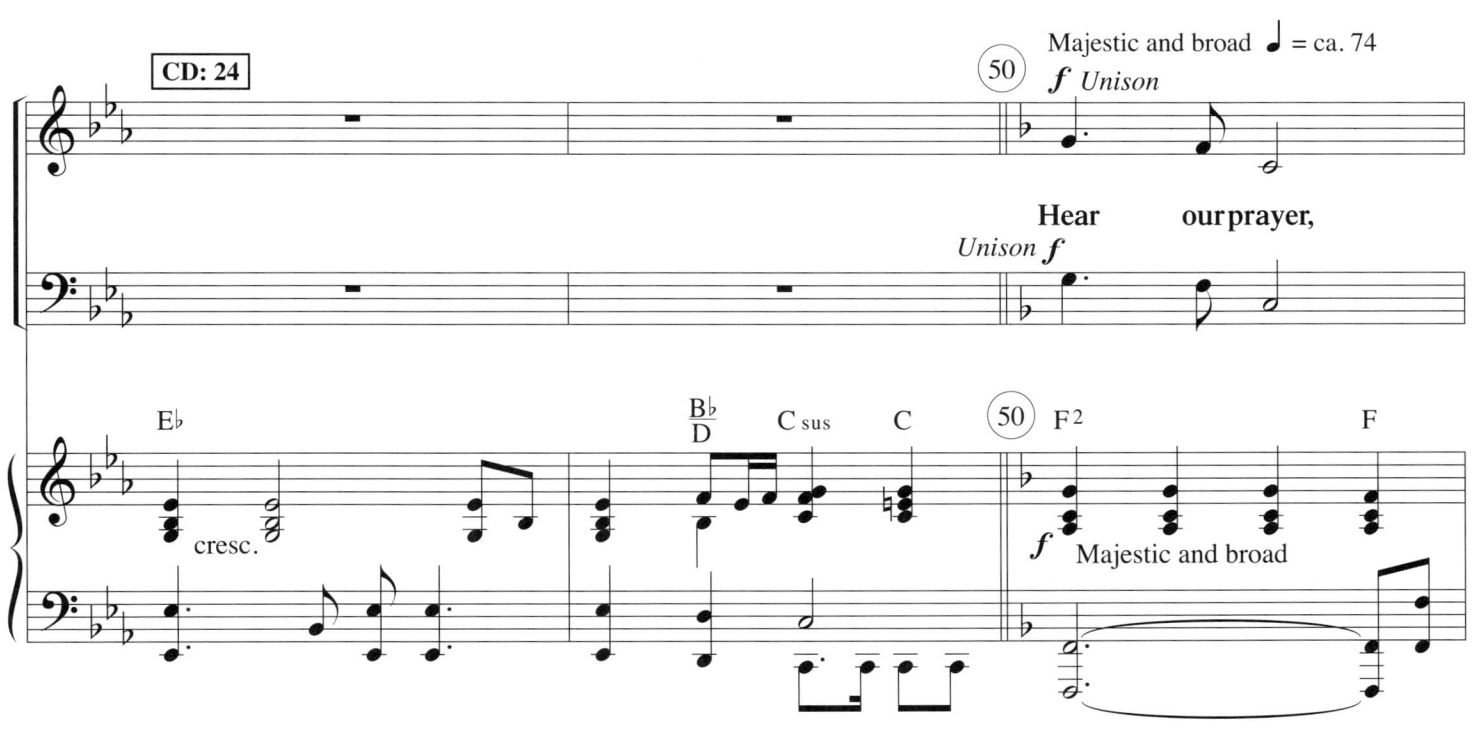

40

God of Our Fathers

DANIEL C. ROBERTS

GEORGE C. WARREN
Arranged by Marty Parks

Arr. © 2003 by PsalmSinger Music (BMI). All rights reserved.
Administered by The Copyright Company, 1025 16th Avenue South, Nashville, TN 37212.

PLEASE NOTE: Copying of this product is NOT covered by CCLI licenses. For CCLI information call 1-800-234-2446.

44

CD: 27

21 *Unison*

Our grate-ful songs be - fore Thy throne a - rise.

Unison

21 D | A/D | G/D | D | D#°7 | E m7 | A sus A | D | C/D | D

26 *mf*

Thy love di - vine hath
Thy love di - vine hath

mf

G | F/D | G | **26** C | A m | A m7 G | C | F

decresc. | *mf*

30

led us in the past. In this free
led, hath led us in the past. In this free

C | G sus | G 7 | C | G m7 | **30** C | A m | A m7

48

NARRATOR *(without music)*: America is many things to many people. Of course, it's the land of the free and the home of the brave. But it's also the country of golden opportunity. America is freedom of expression and freedom of religion. It's bustling cities and quiet little towns; eight-lane interstates and one-lane country roads. *(music begins)* It's baseball and picnics; politcal rallies and revival meetings. It's rock 'n' roll, jazz and folk hymns; Walt Whitman, Mark Twain and Will Rogers; also Betsy Ross, Susan B. Anthony and Sally Ride; George Washington, Thomas Jefferson and Abe Lincoln.

America is unparalled liberty. And it all comes from the hand of God. "Righteousness exalts a nation", the Bible says. "Blessed is the nation whose God is the Lord." *(Proverbs 11:14; Psalm 33:12 NIV)* Let's give Him thanks right now for all He's done.

Doxology
with
His Abundant Blessings

THOMAS KEN
*"His Abundant Blessings"

Attr. to LOUIS BOURGEOIS
Arranged by Marty Parks

*Music by MARTY PARKS. Copyright © 2003 by PsalmSinger Music (BMI). All rights reserved. Administered by The Copyright Company, 1025 16th Avenue South, Nashville, TN 37212.

Arr. © 2003 by PsalmSinger Music (BMI). All rights reserved.
Administered by The Copyright Company, 1025 16th Avenue South, Nashville, TN 37212.

PLEASE NOTE: Copying of this product is NOT covered by CCLI licenses. For CCLI information call 1-800-234-2446.

NARRATOR *(without music)*: Sacrifice has always been a part of our heritage…our heritage as citizens of America and as Christians. We have days set aside to honor and to remember those who have died in military service for the United States, and we know that God's Word says, "I will remember the deeds of the Lord; yes, I will remember your miracles of long ago." *(Psalm 77:11 NIV)*

Often we place flowers or flags on graves to esteem the sacrifice of devoted patriots. And while we ackowledge our great debt to these, we know there was once an even greater sacrifice. *(music begins)* "[Jesus] is the atoning sacrifice for our sins, and not only for ours, but also for the sins of the whole world." *(I John 2:2 NIV)*

No Greater Love

Words and Music by
LEW KING and
BARRY LYALL
Arranged by Marty Parks

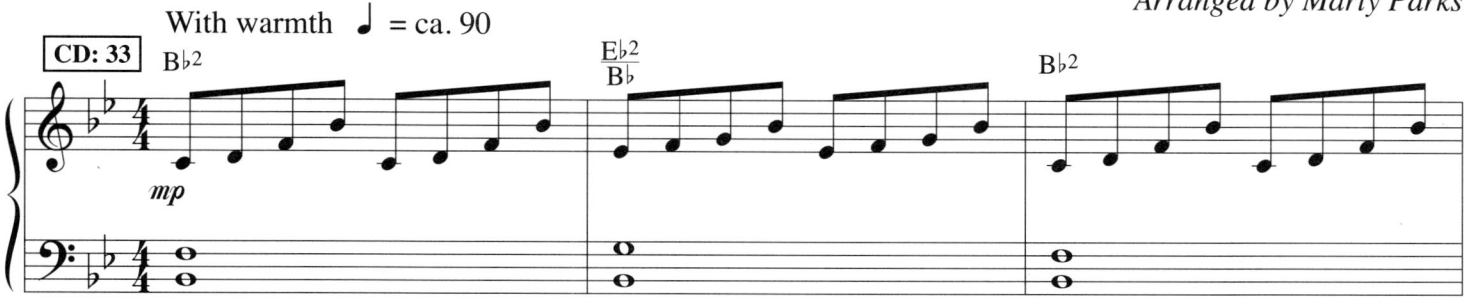

Once on a

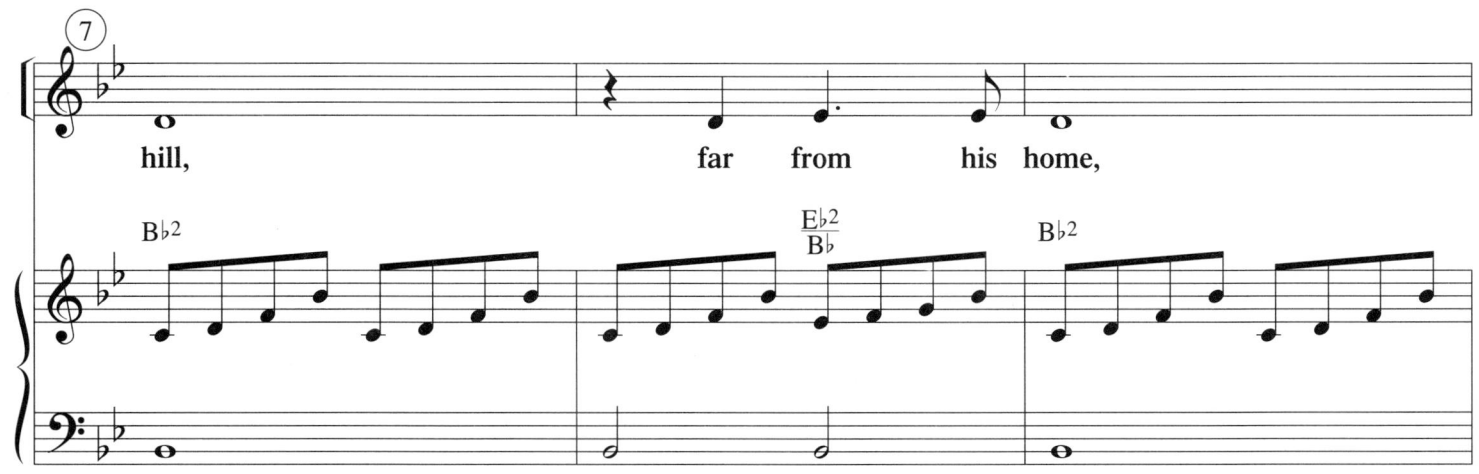

hill, far from his home,

Copyright © 2003 by Pilot Point Music (ASCAP). All rights reserved.
Administered by The Copyright Company, 1025 16th Avenue South, Nashville, TN 37212.

PLEASE NOTE: Copying of this product is NOT covered by CCLI licenses. For CCLI information call 1-800-234-2446.

Measure 61:

Glo - ry prayed a - lone.

The King of Glo - ry, He prayed a -

Gm Eb Fsus

Measure 65:

As morn - ing's light spread to the

lone. As morn - ing's light

F Eb D Gm BbM7/F

Measure 69:

sky, The day had come

spread to the sky, The day had

Eb Eb/G F/A Bb2

Divisi ⑧¹

heart.　　　The　fi - nal　verse

Divisi

F sus　　　　F 7　　Eb　　D ⑧¹ Gm

in　free - dom's　song

Unison

Had　now　been

Unison

Gm　　BbM7/F　　Eb　　　　　　　F/A

⑧⁵

writ - ten　by　His　Son.

CD: 38

⑧⁵ Bb2　　　　　　Eb　　F sus　　　F

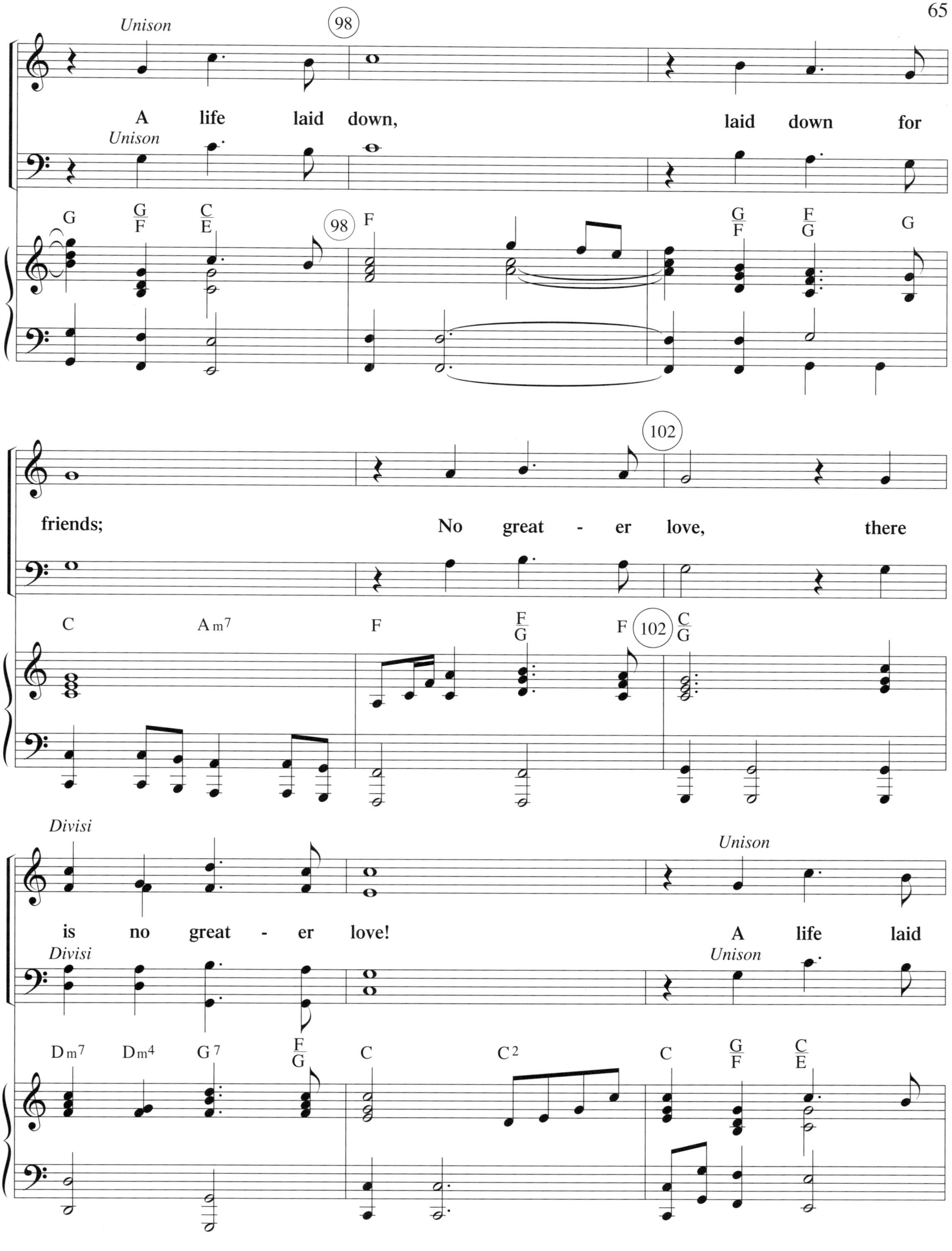
Unison
98
A life laid down, laid down for
Unison
G G/F C/E 98 F G/F F/G G
friends; No great - er love, there
102
C Am7 F F/G F 102 C/G
Divisi
is no great - er love! A life laid
Unison
Divisi
Unison
Dm7 Dm4 G7 F/G C C2 C G/F C/E

Faith of Our Fathers

FREDERICK W. FABER

HENRY F. HEMY
Arranged by Marty Parks

Arr. © 2003 by PsalmSinger Music (BMI). All rights reserved.
Administered by The Copyright Company, 1025 16th Avenue South, Nashville, TN 37212.

PLEASE NOTE: Copying of this product is NOT covered by CCLI licenses. For CCLI information call 1-800-234-2446.

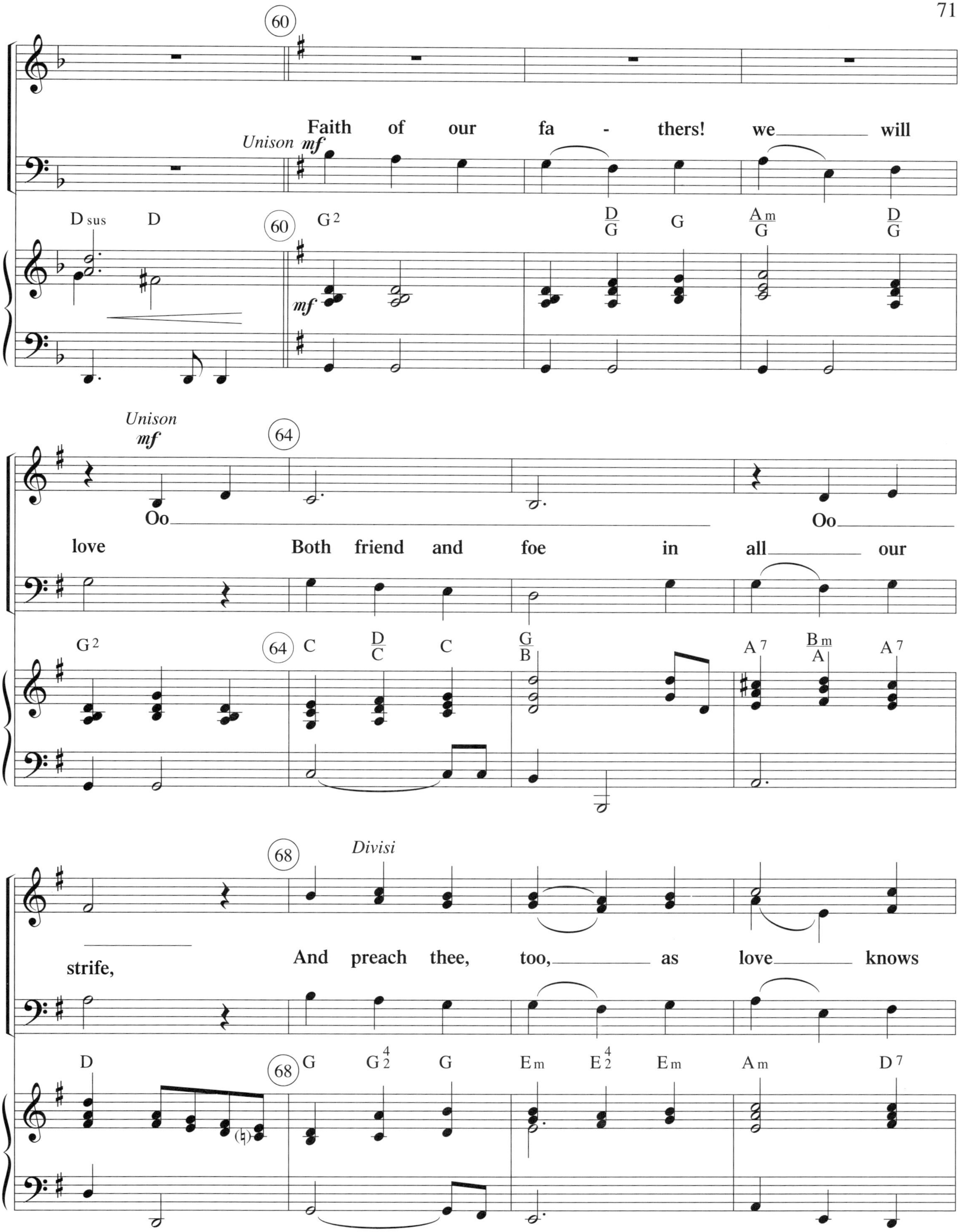
60
Unison mf
Faith of our fa - thers! we will
D sus D G2 D/G G Am/G D/G
mf
Unison mf
64
Oo Oo
love Both friend and foe in all our
G2 C D/C C G/B A7 Bm/A A7
68
Divisi
strife, And preach thee, too, as love knows
D G G4/2 G Em E4/2 Em Am D7
(♮)

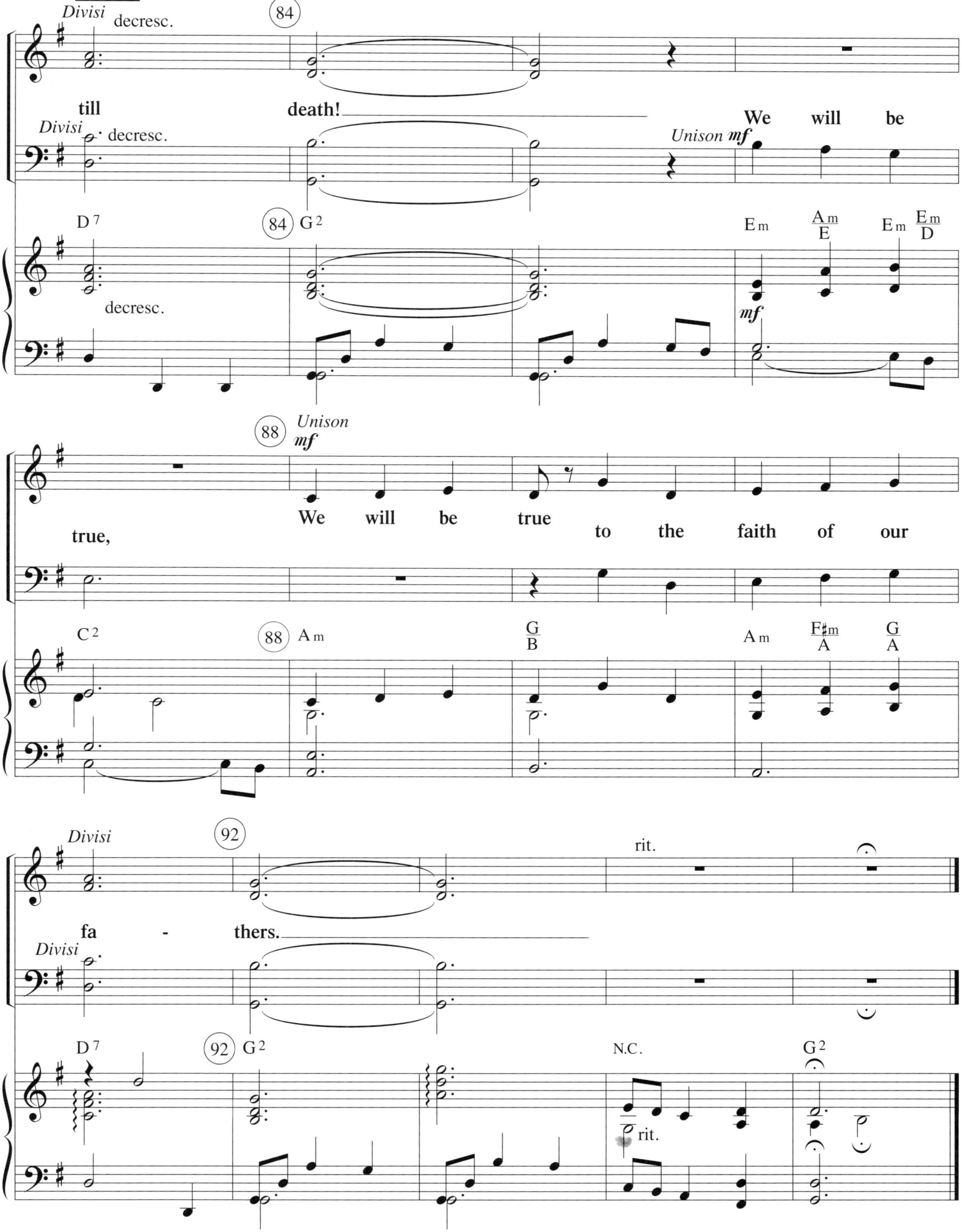
Divisi
decresc.
84
till
death!
We will be
Unison mf
D7
G2
Em
Am/E
Em/D
Unison mf
88
We will be true
true,
to the faith of our
C2
Am
G/B
Am
F♯m/A
G/A
Divisi
92
rit.
fa - thers.
D7
G2
N.C.
rit.

NARRATOR *(without music)*: America! Who would ever have dreamed we'd become what we have? The greatest nation on earth– that's what America is! Problems? Of course. Trying times? You better believe it. Ups and downs? Sure, but it's home…yours and mine. *(music begins)*

So, let's hear it for The United States of America! The Land of the Free! The Home of the Brave! A melting pot of people all wrapped up in red, white and blue. America…my country!

This Is My Country, America
(Reprise)

Words and Music by
MARTY PARKS
Arranged by Marty Parks

Copyright © 2003 by PsalmSinger Music (BMI). All rights reserved.
Administered by The Copyright Company, 1025 16th Avenue South, Nashville, TN 37212.

PLEASE NOTE: Copying of this product is NOT covered by CCLI licenses. For CCLI information call 1-800-234-2446.

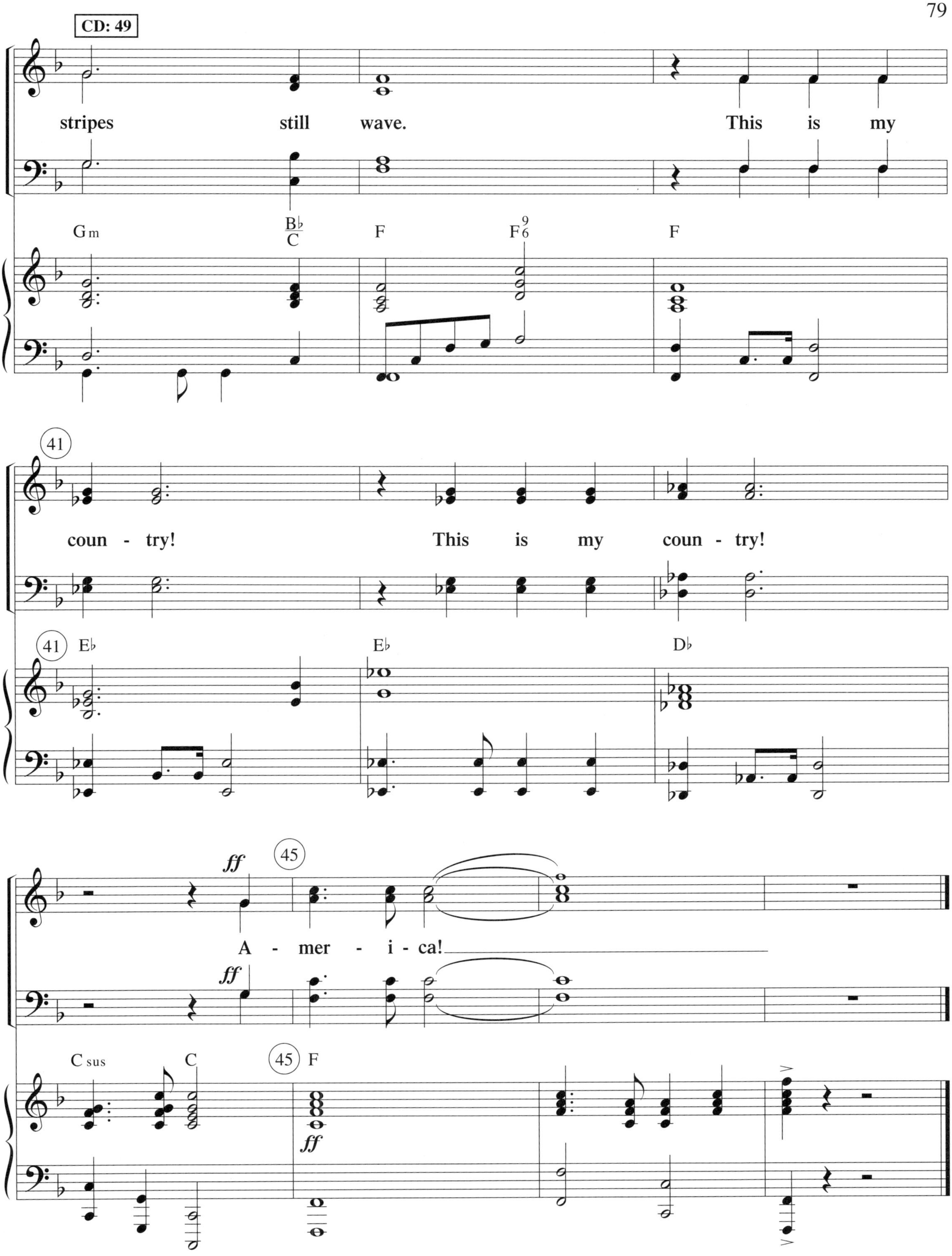
CD: 49
stripes still wave. This is my
Gm
B♭/C
F
F6/9
F
41
coun - try! This is my coun - try!
E♭
E♭
D♭
ff
45
A - mer - i - ca!
Csus
C
F

 **...**

Your source for senior adult choir music

Christmas Musicals

■ *Born Is the King,* arr. Marty Parks   MC-536

■ *Memories of a Merry Christmas,* arr. Marty Parks   MC-524

■ *The Spirit of Christmas,* arr. Marty Parks   MC-509

Thanksgiving Musical

■ *Count Your Blessings,*
     Sue C. Smith and Russell Mauldin   MB-755

Non-Seasonal Musical

■ *The Gospel Never Changes,*
     Martha Bolton and Marty Parks   MB-728

Choral Collections

■ *Bless That Wonderful Name,* arr. Marty Parks   MB-818

■ *Jubilee,* arr. Mosie Lister   MB-704

Lillenas.com